Recipe Book

The Best Food Recipes That Are Delicious Healthy Great For Energy And Easy To Make

By Ace McCloud
Copyright © 2014

Disclaimer

The information provided in this book is designed to provide helpful information on the subjects discussed. This book is not meant to be used, nor should it be used, to diagnose or treat any medical condition. For diagnosis or treatment of any medical problem, consult your own physician. The publisher and author are not responsible for any specific health or allergy needs that may require medical supervision and are not liable for any damages or negative consequences from any treatment, action, application or preparation, to any person reading or following the information in this book. Any references included are provided for informational purposes only. Readers should be aware that any websites or links listed in this book may change.

Table of Contents

Introduction 6

Chapter 1- Welcome the Morning with Quick, Energy filled Breakfasts............................... 11

Chapter 2 - Energy Lunches to Prepare and Eat at Home, Work or School 25

Chapter 3 - Homemade Energy Snacks 34

Chapter 4 - Easy, Quick and Healthy Dinners 45

Conclusion 70

My Other Books and Audio Books 71

Be sure to check out my website for all my Books and Audio books.

www.AcesEbooks.com

Introduction

I want to thank you and congratulate you for buying the book, "Recipe Book: The Best Food Recipes That Are Delicious, Healthy, Great For Energy And Easy To Make"

This book contains delicious recipes that are easy to make, nutritious and energizing.

Several different types of food provide energy for the body, and some are better than others. Those foods earmarked as "energy" or "power" foods slowly release energy to the body for a continuous supply. Other foods give the body a big burst of energy, but that energy then dwindles quickly and can leave you fatigued. This book will acquaint you with recipes using those "energy" or "power" foods. The recipes in this book are easy to make, healthy and delicious in addition to supplying the body with the energy it needs to function at top form.

Think of your body being run by a fine tuned engine, just like your car. Your car needs fuel to run well. If you give it the wrong fuel, things start to go wrong. The injectors may be clogged; the pistons may stick and the engine can just stop running all together. Eating the wrong kinds of food clogs your arteries, gums up your digestive system and can lead to a variety of negative consequences.

Fatigue during the day is often the result of eating the wrong types of foods. The video, <u>Fatigued- Get More ENERGY from the Foods You Eat</u> by Dr. Luke Pocock, will help you see how eating the right foods will give you the most energy.

The body produces energy by turning what you eat into glucose. Carbohydrates are substances that are easily turned into this glucose, or sugar, but you have to be careful. Complex carbohydrates, like whole grains, are the ones that keep energy levels even while simple carbohydrates, like processed sugar, give you immediate energy that plummets soon after leaving you tired. If you put the wrong type of gas in your car, you are asking for trouble. The same thing goes with your body.

The foods that give the body energy are also very healthy. They fight disease, provide fiber to the digestive system and help the metabolism to run at high speed.

VITAMINS

Leafy greens are an energy food that supplies Vitamin C and Vitamin D, which are important for maintaining energy. These greens include spinach, kale, chard, Brussels sprouts, cabbage and collard greens. Notice lettuce is not on the list. Lettuce is mostly water and iceberg lettuce has the least vitamin value of all the lettuces. You do get some vitamin value with Romain and other types of lettuce.

Broccoli has important antioxidants called glucosinolates, which fight cancer. Red bell peppers contain loads of Vitamin C and other substances that fight fatigue.

COMPLEX CARBOHYDRATES
Whole grains are energy inducing because the carbohydrates release slowly and give the body energy for a long period of time. Whole wheat bread is better than white bread because the white variety contains refined flour; a simple carbohydrate. After eating white bread you may crash after about 30 minutes while whole grains keep you going strong. Brown rice is better than white rice in the same manner. Other sources of complex carbohydrates are barley, oats and quinoa. Sweet potatoes are another complex carbohydrate that is a real energy supply.

PROTEIN
Lean meats including chicken, turkey and lean cuts of beef and pork are filled with protein. Protein aids other foods that give the body energy and help with endurance. Protein helps you feel full longer and is great for building and repairing muscle. Red meat is a source of iron and B Vitamins, which are used to develop good muscle tone. The amino acid, tyrosine, is found in meat and it helps fight fatigue. Grass fed red meat animals is better for you because they have about four times the Vitamin E, three times the Omega-E's and 10 times more Beta Carotene that

regular meat. Grass fed beef is also lower in saturated fats.

Nuts, including almonds, walnuts, pecans and cashews provide a great deal of protein. They also contain the co enzyme Q10 that is thought to help cells produce energy. Peanut butter is another source of good protein. Eggs are the perfect food. They contain the same protein, Vitamin B and Iron as red meat. There is little evidence that eggs cause your arteries to clog as long as they are eaten in moderation. Beans, or legumes, like kidney beans, black beans, canellini beans and garbanzo beans and lentils are another source of protein that lends endurance when eaten with energy foods. They also contain iron and Vitamin B plus fiber that is good for digestion.

OTHER ENERGY LADEN FOODS
Salmon contains fatty acids that regulate blood sugar. Salmon is also called brain food because it supplies needed nutrients for brain cells to thrive and grow.

Fruits are another power food that most people enjoy eating. Bananas contain potassium and produce glucose that supplies energy to the body. If you feel fatigued, eat a banana to give yourself some quick energy. Apples provide fiber, vitamin C and fructose, which is a sugar that processes into energy. Watermelon is full of potassium, which provides fluids to the body. Blueberries contain antioxidants and also provide massive amounts of energy.

Learn more about how your body uses the foods you eat to produce energy and what you should and shouldn't eat by watching the YouTube video, Eating for Energy by Yuri Elkaim.

The following chapters contain recipes containing these energy foods and more. The chapters are split into types of meals which include breakfast, lunch, dinner, snacks and deserts. All the recipes are healthy, easy to create and great for your energy levels!

Chapter 1- Welcome the Morning with Quick, Energy filled Breakfasts

It's a good idea to never skip any meals, because eating at regular intervals supplies the body with a continuous source of energy. Skipping breakfast allows blood sugar to go down by mid-morning which can lead to a decrease in your energy levels.

A power breakfast consists of protein, fiber and vitamins. Stay away from refined sugar because it will spike your blood sugar way up and in a few hours it will crash. Pancakes and syrup or sugary cereal are not good ideas. Orange juice supplies the body with a good dose of Vitamin C. Other vitamins are supplied by the food you eat for breakfast. The following are a few power breakfast entrées that will get you through to lunch without getting drowsy.

Muffins and scones and other types of bread make for a nutritious energy breakfast as long as they are not made completely with refined or white flour. The following recipes are simple and you can last for several days. The muffins or scones can also be frozen for whenever they are needed.

BREAKFAST MUFFINS

These muffins do contain some white flour, but there is so many other good things in them that the white flour isn't that bad. This recipe contains yogurt, which is another high energy food full of active cultures that keep the stomach and digestive system working well.

Ingredients:
1/2 cup whole wheat flour
3/4 cup all-purpose flour
2 tablespoons baking soda
1/8 teaspoon salt
1/4 teaspoon ground cinnamon
1/8 teaspoon ground nutmeg
1/4 cup brown sugar
2 tablespoons wheat germ
3/4 cup raisins
8 ounces plain low-fat yogurt
4 tablespoons Canola or vegetable oil
1 egg
1/2 tablespoon orange zest
3 tablespoons fresh orange juice

Directions
Preheat the oven to 400 degrees F and line 12 muffin tins with paper liners.

In a large mixing bowl, sift the two different flours, baking soda, salt, cinnamon and nutmeg together. Add the brown sugar, wheat germ and the raisins. Form a mound in the bowl with the dry ingredients and hollow out the center. It should look like a volcano. This is called making a well.

In a small bowl, whisk the yogurt, oil, egg, orange zest and orange juice. Pour it in the hole of the well.

Gradually incorporate some of the dry ingredients at the edge of the well into the liquid ingredients and mix with a fork. Keep adding more and more, little by little until it is all incorporated. Do not over stir. It just needs to be moist.

Fill the muffin cups 3/4 full. Place the muffin tin in the oven and bake for 15 to 20 minutes or until a toothpick poked in the middle of one of the muffins comes out clean.

Cool for 5 or 6 minutes and turn out onto a wire rack. Store in an air tight container or freeze in freezer bags.

BLUEBERRY LEMON ENERGY SCONES

Blueberries are one of the energy foods because of their antioxidants. Other ingredients like oats, flaxseed, yogurt and honey make these scones a delicious and healthy breakfast.

Ingredients:
1-1/4 cup whole grain flour
1 cup ground whole oats
1/2 cup nonfat dry milk
2 tablespoons ground flaxseed
2 teaspoons baking powder
1/2 teaspoon baking soda
1/8 teaspoon salt

1 cup low-fat blueberry flavored yogurt or plain yogurt
1/4 cup honey
2 tablespoons canola oil
2 tablespoons fresh lemon juice
2 teaspoons lemon zest
1-1/2 cup blueberries

Directions:
Preheat the oven to 400 degrees F and lightly spray a cookie sheet with non-stick coating.

In a large bowl, whisk the flour, oats, dry milk, flaxseed, baking powder, baking soda and salt together. In a smaller bowl, whisk the yogurt, honey, oil, juice of the lemon and lemon zest.

Make mound with the dry ingredients and hollow out the center. Scrape the yogurt mixture in the center and gradually stir it all together so that all the ingredients are moistened. Add the blueberries and carefully fold them in being careful not to break them.

Drop the batter on the prepared cookie sheets by scooping out with a 1/4 cup measuring cup spacing them about 1 inch apart. It should make about 10 to 12 scones.

Bake for 12 to 15 minutes or until the scones lightly brown and firm. Serve warm or cold.

PEANUT BUTTER AND BANANA BAGLE

Bananas contain potassium and give you extra energy while peanut butter is full of protein. Put it all on a whole grain bagel and you have a breakfast that will have you jumping through hoops until noon. You can eat this as you go out the door to catch the bus or drive to work.

Ingredients:
1/2 whole grain bagel
2 teaspoons peanut butter or other nut flavored butter
1/2 banana, sliced

Directions:
Spread the peanut butter on the bagel and slice a half of banana on top.

NUTRITIOUS AND ENERGY LADEN BREAKFAST SANDWICH

Breakfast sandwiches are popular at fast food restaurants, but they hold no candle to this healthy sandwich. It is an open face sandwich, which means you only consume half of an English muffin and that cuts down on the carbs. It includes a hard-boiled egg for protein and spinach that contains iron. The recipe makes two sandwiches.

Ingredients:
1 whole wheat English muffin cut in half
1/2 cup fresh spinach leaves, cooked and squeezed dry
2 slices of tomato
2 hard-boiled eggs, thinly sliced

1 teaspoon light mayonnaise
a pinch of salt per half

Directions:
Place the muffin halves on a baking sheet covered with foil and top with the cooked dry spinach and one tomato slice per muffin. Place the egg slices in a spiral on top starting at the outside edges and working toward the center. Drop a dollop of mayonnaise on top and spread over the sandwich

Place the cookie sheet under the broiler for about 2 to 3 minutes letting the mayonnaise brown. Remove and eat.

BLT FOR BREAKFAST
You use Canadian bacon for this sandwich, which is very lean and healthier than regular bacon. This recipe makes one or two portions depending on if you want it to be open faced or a regular sandwich. If you want to make two, you need to double all the ingredients.

Ingredients:
1 whole grain English muffin
1 teaspoon low-fat mayonnaise
1 slice Canadian bacon
1/4 cup shredded Romaine lettuce
1 slice tomato

Directions:

Toast the English muffin and top it with the mayonnaise. In a frying pan, heat the Canadian bacon and when heated through, place it on top on side of the muffin. Sprinkle on the lettuce and place the tomato slice on top.

SALMON AND EGGS SANDWICH
Smoked salmon is full of Omega-3's and protein. The egg whites add even more protein. This recipe will keep you full all the way to lunch. This recipe makes 1 sandwich.

Ingredients:
1/2 teaspoon olive oil
1 tablespoon red onion, finely chopped
2 large egg whites, beaten
pinch of salt
pinch of pepper
1 ounce smoked salmon
1 slice tomato
1 whole wheat English Muffin, split and toasted

Directions:
Turn the burner on medium high under a small frying pan and let it heat up. Add the oil and cook the onion stirring until it becomes translucent, about 1 minute. Add the egg whites, salt and pepper. Stir constantly until the egg whites set, about 30 to 40 seconds.

Place half of the toasted English muffin on a serving plate. Top with egg whites, salmon and the tomato and place the other half of the muffin on top.

WHOLE GRAIN WAFFLES WITH RICOTTA AND FRUIT

If you still have that urge to have something like pancakes and syrup, this recipe will stop the craving and provide you with a healthy breakfast. The ricotta cheese is a great source of protein and you can use any type of fruit: fresh, frozen, or canned. Thaw the frozen fruit and drain and get canned fruit in its own juice and drain it too. Peaches, pineapple, strawberries and blueberries are good fruits to try. This recipe makes one serving.

Ingredients:
1 whole wheat frozen waffle
1/2 cup part-skim ricotta cheese
1/2 cup fruit

Directions:
Toast the waffle and lay it on a plate. Spread with the ricotta cheese and top with fruit.

OVERNIGHT BANANA NUT OATMEAL

Oatmeal is a great breakfast cereal that sticks to your ribs and keeps you from getting hungry in the middle of the morning. Pair it with bananas and nuts and you have a real treat that is filling and healthy. Make the oatmeal the previous night, put it in mason jars and leave it in the refrigerator overnight. In the morning take out the jars, empty the contents in a bowl and microwave for a quick breakfast. This recipe makes 2 large servings or 4 smaller servings.

Ingredients:
1 cup steel-cut oats
2-1/2 cups water
pinch of salt
1-1/2 bananas, peeled and mashed
1/8 cup packed brown sugar
1/2 tablespoon lemon juice
2 to 4 – 12 ounce canning jars
1/2 cup milk
1/2 cup chopped walnuts.

Directions:
In a saucepan, mix the oats, water and salt. Bring the ingredients to a boil and once it does, reduce it to a simmer. Cover with a lid and cook 10 minutes. The oatmeal will be watery. Turn off the heat and stir in the mashed bananas, brown sugar and lemon juice. Pour into 4 canning jars equally, put on the lids and screw them down tight. Cool on the counter top and place in the refrigerator before going to bed.

In the morning pour the ingredients of each jar into a bowl and add 1 tablespoon milk and 1 tablespoon chopped nuts. You can sprinkle the oatmeal with more brown sugar on top if desired. Put in each serving in the microwave for about 2 minutes, cool 1 minute. You can add a few more slices of fresh banana on top.

SCRAMBLED SPINACH AND CHEESE EGGS

This is a quick breakfast that has a great deal of protein in it to keep you going through your day. This recipe is for 1 serving.

Ingredients:
1/2 cup fresh spinach
1 teaspoon olive oil
2 eggs or 1 egg and 2 egg whites
1 pinch of salt and pepper
1/4 cup cheese, shredded

Directions:
In a frying pan, cook the baby spinach in the oil just long enough to heat it up and wilt the leaves.

In a small bowl, add the egg and whisk it well with salt and pepper. Place in the frying pan with the spinach and scramble. Sprinkle with cheese and serve.

CINNAMON LACED COTTAGE CHEESE DIP WITH APPLE

Cottage cheese is a very good source of protein and it goes down very well in the morning. Sweeten it up with some cinnamon and apple. This recipe serves 2.

Ingredients:
3/4 cup low-fat cottage cheese

1 teaspoon cinnamon, ground
1 apple, peeled and sliced
1 tablespoon lemon juice

Directions:
In a bowl, stir the cottage cheese and cinnamon together.

Squeeze the lemon juice in a pie pan and add the peeled sliced apple. Toss to coat so that the apple will not turn brown. Place the coated apples on a paper towel for a few minutes to dry off and then place in a small bowl. Take the apple and dip it in the cottage cheese mix for a dipping breakfast treat the kids will love. You can also just mix it all together in a bowl to eat.

QUINOA YOGURT PARFAIT
Quinoa is a grain that has protein and yogurt has active cultures that keep the body healthy. This recipe makes 1 parfait, but your family will want one too, so make enough for all.

Ingredients:
1/2 cup quinoa, cooked
6 ounces nonfat yogurt
1 small apple, chopped
dash of ground cinnamon
dash of ground ginger

Directions:

Pour one third of the quinoa at the bottom of a glass serving dish. Layer the quinoa with some of the yogurt, some apple and a little ground cinnamon and ginger. Then make another layer, cool in the refrigerator overnight and serve in the morning.

BERRY SMOOTHIE
Smoothies are great when you are on the run. You can just take it with you and drink it on the way to work.

Ingredients:
1/2 cup skim or soy milk
6 ounces non-fat vanilla Greek Yogurt
1/4 cup frozen berries
2 ice cubes or 1/8 cup ice chips

Directions:
Place all ingredients in the blender and blend it until it is a milk shake consistency.

You can also add a scoop of protein powder into this smoothie to make it even more nutritious.

BREAKFAST BURRITO
This recipe has beans, spinach, eggs and all kinds of good things to give you an energy boost in the morning. It makes 6 servings.

Ingredients:
1 – 15 ounce can black beans, rinsed and drained

1/3 cup jarred salsa
1-1/2 cups fresh spinach, chopped
3 large eggs and 3 egg whites
1/2 cup onion, chopped
1/4 cup cilantro, chopped
1/4 teaspoon chili powder
1/8 teaspoon salt
6 whole wheat tortillas
3/4 cup shredded Cheddar

Directions:
In a saucepan, mix the beans and salsa. Cook the mixture over medium heat and stir every once and a while until warm.

Coat a nonstick skillet with non-stick spray and set over medium heat. Once hot, add the spinach and cook until it wilts, about 3 minutes.

Wisk the eggs and egg whites in a bowl and add the onion, cilantro, chili powder and salt. Add to the wilted spinach in the skillet and scramble until eggs are set, about 2 minutes.

Place tortillas in the microwave individually between two damp paper towels and microwave on high for one minute. Place warmed tortillas on a cutting board. Sprinkle on equal amounts of cheese and divide the bean mixture among the tortillas. Top with the egg mixture. Fold the short edges over the filling, roll and serve.

These breakfast recipes will give you excellent energy. View this YouTube video, [High Energy Breakfasts For Kids & Teens](#) by Lisa De Fazio, for suggestions that kids of all ages will love.

Chapter 2 - Energy Lunches to Prepare and Eat at Home, Work or School

A heavy lunch leaves you feeling tired out and lethargic, but eating too little for lunch can do the same thing. You have to get the right balance and eat the best foods that will give you energy. A trip to the local fast food restaurant may stop the hunger and energize you for a little while, but when 2 or 3 o'clock comes around, you might be snoozing on your desk.

Avoid eating more than 1000 calories for lunch. If you need a mid-morning or mid-afternoon snack to stay full, choose a healthy snack instead of something sugary or carbohydrate laden. Avoid lunches that are heavy on carbohydrates. Pasta and bread might not be the best idea. Protein and salads are the "go to" dishes for an energy lunch, although a quick whole grain sandwich will also work well for those that brown bag their lunch.

See the YouTube video, Pack Healthy Lunches | Whole Kids | Whole Foods Market from WholefoodsMarket and The Container Store, for some more ideas on healthy energy lunches.

The following recipes are lunches that are easy to make and take along to the office or school. They will keep you feeling full all afternoon and will also keep your energy levels up so you can be productive.

CALIFORNIA TURKY CLUB

This recipe makes one sandwich that uses whole wheat bread and turkey bacon, better choices for energy besides white bread and regular pork bacon. The avocado is also a high energy food that will keep fatigue away.

Ingredients:
2 slices whole-grain bread
2 tablespoons mashed avocado
2 slices of turkey bacon
3 slices deli turkey
3 lettuce leaves
2 tomato slices

Directions:
Toast the bread and spread the avocado on to one piece of the toast.

Cook the bacon and when it is crisp, drain it on paper towels. Assemble the sandwich by placing the turkey slices on the toast without the avocado followed by the lettuce leaves and tomato slices. Place the turkey bacon on top and cover with the avocado spread toast.

ROAST BEEF AND HORSERADISH WRAP

Using a tortilla to make a wrap avoids the use of processed white bread or large quantities of any type of bread. Use a whole wheat tortilla instead of the flour types. This recipe makes one wrap.

Ingredients:
2 teaspoons light mayonnaise
1/2 teaspoon prepared horseradish
1 whole wheat tortilla
1 large leaf of Romaine lettuce
3 slices of roast beef
1/8 cup tomato, chopped

Directions:
In a small bowl, combine the mayo with the horseradish. Spread the mixture on one half of the tortilla. Place a leaf of lettuce in the middle of the tortilla. Top with the slices of beef and a slice of tomato. Fold in the outer edges and roll.

You can adjust the amount of horseradish you put in the wrap. Some people like a light touch of horseradish while others like their eyes and nose to run.

CHICKEN AND PINEAPPLE SANDWICH
This sandwich is better eaten right away while it is warm, but it isn't bad packed in a lunch. You can always put the chicken and pineapple in a microwave safe dish and microwave it and place it in the roll at the office. This recipe makes 4 sandwiches, so it makes for a delicious Saturday or Sunday.

Ingredients:
4 chicken breast halves, skinless and boneless
Teriyaki sauce

4 fresh pineapple slices cut 1/2 inch thick
1 fresh jalapeño pepper, seeded and sliced thin
4 slices Swiss cheese
4 whole-wheat rolls
1/2 medium onion, thinly sliced

Directions:
Put chicken breasts in a closable storage bag and pour enough Teriyaki sauce over top to cover. Close and put in the refrigerator for 30 minutes to 1/2 hour.

Take the chicken from the bag and put it on the grill for about 4 to 5 minutes on one side. Flip the chicken breast over and place one slice of cheese per breast on the cooked side. Grill until the breast is cooked through and brown. Discard the rest of the Teriyaki sauce.

Add the pineapple slices to the grill. Open the rolls and put them face down on the grill to toast. Cook the pineapple slices 2 minutes on each side until they are caramelized. Place the chicken breast on the roll topped with the pineapple. Sprinkle with the jalapeño and onion. This is optional because the sandwich is good with or without it.

PITA FILLED WITH WHITE BEANS AND PESTO
This is a flavorful lunch that can be considered a sandwich and it packs energy with the protein filled beans. The pesto gives this lunch a strong flavor that

is very delicious. The beans are a good source of protein. This recipe makes 1 pita.

Ingredients:
2/3 cup canned white beans, rinsed and drained
1/2 cup diced tomatoes
2 teaspoons pesto
1 whole grain pita

Directions:
In a small bowl, mix the beans, tomatoes and pesto. Fill the pita. You can add a little lettuce and make your own pesto or use jarred pesto.

MEXICAN ROLL-UP

This dish brings the flavors of the Southwest and Mexico to your lunch table. You can make it at work by bringing the ingredients and warming them in the microwave and then spreading them in a tortilla. The beans are your protein and spinach leaves give you iron. This recipe makes 1 roll-up.

Ingredients:
1 large whole grain tortilla
3/4 cup canned refried beans
4 tablespoons salsa
1/4 cup low-fat shredded Cheddar
4 spinach leaves, chopped

Directions:

Place the beans in a microwave safe dish and microwave to warm them.

Spread the beans on the tortilla and top with the Cheddar while warm. Layer on the salsa and spinach leaves and roll.

You can spread a little low-fat sour cream on the tortilla before spreading the beans if desired.

BERRY, CHICKEN AND GOAT CHEESE SALAD

The berries in this salad are packed with vitamins and the goat cheese is a source of protein as is the chicken. The salad is more filling than you may think and can keep you going until dinner. This recipe makes 1 salad.

Ingredients:
Salad
1 tablespoon pecans
3 cups fresh spinach
1/2 cup strawberries, halved
1/2 cup blueberries
1/2 cup fresh pineapple, chopped
1 skinless chicken breast, grilled
1 tablespoon goat cheese crumbles
Dressing
1/4 cup sliced strawberries
1 tablespoon orange juice, squeezed
1-1/2 teaspoons red wine vinegar

1/2 teaspoon orange zest
1/2 teaspoon sugar
2 tablespoons non-fat Greek yogurt
1 pinch of salt

Directions:
Begin by making the dressing by placing all ingredients in a blender and blending until smooth.

Preheat the oven to 400 degrees F. Place the pecans on a cookie sheet covered with foil and toast for 2 minutes. Take out of the oven and set aside.

In a bowl, toss the spinach, berries, pineapple with drizzles of the dressing. Divide between 2 dinner plates and thinly slice the chicken placing half on each plate. Sprinkle the the nuts and goat cheese crumbles and serve.

TUNA AND BEAN SALAD
This salad has staying power from the tuna and cannellini beans. It makes 4 servings, so invite your friends over for a light, delicious and energy laden lunch.

Ingredients:
2 – 6 ounce cans of tuna, drained
1 – 15 ounce can cannellini beans, rinsed and drained
10 cherry tomatoes, quartered
4 green onions, sliced
2 tablespoons olive oil

2 tablespoons fresh lemon juice
1/8 teaspoon salt
1/8 teaspoon fresh ground pepper

Directions:
In a bowl, mix all the ingredients to combine. Serve on a large lettuce leaf or bed of baby spinach leaves.

SALMON SALAD
This salad is high in Omega-3's, which give you energy. It also has walnuts, honey and mustard that help supply energy to the body. This recipe makes 4 servings.

Ingredients:
8 cups mixed baby greens
1/4 cup walnuts, chopped (you can use pecans, almonds, or any type of nut)
1 tablespoon olive oil
1 teaspoon walnut oil (omit if using another nut and double the olive oil)
2 teaspoons Balsamic vinegar
1/8 teaspoon sea salt
3/4 pound salmon fillet
1/4 cup honey
2 tablespoons Dijon mustard

Directions:
Heat a skillet over medium heat and toast the walnuts with a spray of butter flavored non-stick spray. Toast

while stirring constantly for about 1 minute and set aside.

Heat the same skillet over medium heat and put 1/2 tablespoon of the olive oil in. Add half of the greens and cook 1 minute to wilt them slightly. Place them in a large salad bowl and continue with more oil and more greens. Toss with the walnut oil, vinegar and salt.

Preheat a broiler to high. Place the salmon, skin side down, on an oven proof dish.

In a bowl, mix the honey and mustard. Brush this on the salmon and broil 8 to 10 minutes flipping after half the time has elapsed. Remove from the broiler and cut in 4 equal servings. Place the greens on 4 plates and top with the salmon and sprinkle with toasted nuts.

Fill up with these nutritious and healthy energy producing lunch ideas. Eat them at home, at the office or at school to get through the day with gusto.

Chapter 3 - Homemade Energy Snacks

In order to keep blood sugar at a level rate, and keep energy flowing to the body, it might be necessary to eat something small between meals. The following snacks will do just that and they are nutritious and they help give you a boost of energy.

Sometimes you just want a treat to delight the taste buds and some of these snacks are sweet and delicious, but still healthy.

PROTIEN PACKED BARS

FUDGEY NO-BAKE PROTEIN BARS
Chocolate lovers will love these bars for a quick pick up. The flax seed, protein powder and almond meal all pack a punch of energy and there is no sugar in this sweet treat because stevia is used.

Ingredients:
1/2 cup almond butter
1/2 cup of water
1/4 cup raw cocoa powder
1/4 cup ground flax seed
1 cup chocolate protein powder
6 packets of Stevia sweetener
1/8 teaspoon vanilla
2 tablespoons almond meal

Directions:

In a large bowl, mix the almond butter with the water until well blended. Add the cocoa powder, flax seed, protein powder, Stevia and vanilla and combine using a wooden spoon until a thick dough forms. Roll the dough into a rope shape with the hands and cut it in 16 pieces.

Place the almond meal in a bowl and press each piece into it. Place on a wax paper covered baking sheet and press lightly with the fingers to form a bar. Place the bars in an airtight container and store in the refrigerator.

HONEY AND ALMOND PROTEIN BARS

These bars might seem a little complicated and have more ingredients than you would want, but they are so delicious and pack so much energy laden ingredients in them that you won't mind the extra effort once you try them. Some of the ingredients like the Turbinado sugar, which is a raw cane sugar that has a molasses flavor, can be found in Health food stores.

Ingredients:
1 cup old-fashion rolled oats (do not use quick oats)
1/4 cup almonds, slivered
1/4 cup sunflower seed (without the hulls)
1 tablespoon flax seed
1 cup unsweetened whole-grain puffed cereal (Use Kashi 7 Whole Grain Puffs)
1/3 cup dried currants or raisins

1/3 cup dried apricots, chopped
1/4 cup creamy almond butter
1/4 cup Turbinado sugar
1/4 cup honey
1/2 teaspoon vanilla
1/8 teaspoon salt

Directions:
Preheat the oven to 350 degrees Fahrenheit and coat an 8-inch square pan with non-stick cooking spray.

Use a rimmed baking sheet to toast the rolled oats, almonds, sunflower seeds and flax seeds and bake until the oats are lightly toasted. Give the pan a stir halfway through at about 10 minutes. Pour the toasted ingredients into a large bowl.

Add the cereal, raisins, and apricots to the bowl and combine well.

In a saucepan, mix the almond butter, sugar, honey, vanilla and salt and place over medium-low stirring constantly about 2 to 5 minutes or until the mixture starts to bubble.

While still hot, pour the almond butter mixture over the dry ingredients in the bowl and mix with a spatula. Press into the 8-inch square pan. Spray hands with non-stick spray and press the mixture down packing it into the pan. Refrigerate until it all is firm, about 1/2 hour, and cut into 8 bars.

Store in an airtight container in the refrigerator.

CHOCOLATE CHERRY POWER BARS
This bar is like eating Black Forest Cake. They do have some sugar in the mini chocolate chips, but there are so many other good things in them, you can have them every once in a while.

Ingredients:
2-1/2 cup unsweetened puffed wheat cereal
1/2 cup finely chopped pecan halves
1/2 cup almonds, slivered
1/4 cup dried cherries
1 – 1/2 tablespoons sesame seeds
1 – 1/2 tablespoon ground flax seed
1/2 cup honey
1/2 teaspoon vanilla
1/8 teaspoon salt
1/2 cup mini semisweet chocolate chips

Directions:
Place the oven rack in the lower third of the oven and preheat to 300 degrees Fahrenheit. Line an 8-inch square pan with parchment paper and let it overhang the pan on two opposite side so you are able to pull the bars out when done.

In a large bowl, mix the cereal, pecans, almonds, cherries, sesame seed, and flax seed.

In a saucepan warm the honey, vanilla and salt over medium, stirring constantly, until the honey is fluid and salt is dissolved. Pour over the dry mixture in the bowl and fold in with a spatula until well coated. Let sit 5 minutes to cool. Fold in the chocolate chips and place in the prepared pan.

Using a fork, press the ingredients in the pan firmly. Bake about 30 to 35 minutes, until the top is browned. Run a knife around the sides opposite the parchment paper hanging out and let cool about 1 hour. Take hold of the two sides of parchment paper and lift the bars out of the pan. Peel off the paper and cut into 16 bars.

Store in an airtight container.

For another great energy bar recipes using dates, see this YouTube video, High Energy Raw Power Bars Recipe by Power of Food.

SWEET TREATS FOR DESSERT OR SNACKS

BLUEBERRY WHITE CHOCOLATE GINGER COOKIES

This recipe does use all-purpose flour, but it also uses wheat germ, ginger, oats and blueberries, all of which are great energy foods. The cookies taste really good too and there is only 115 calories per cookie.

Ingredients:

1 cup all-purpose flour
1/4 cup wheat germ
1/2 teaspoon baking soda
1/4 teaspoon salt
1/4 teaspoon ginger
1 large egg
3/4 cup dark brown sugar, packed
1/3 cup vegetable oil
1 teaspoon vanilla
1/2 cup old fashion rolled oats (not instant or quick)
2 ounces white chocolate, chopped
1/3 cup dried blueberries
1/4 cup crystallized ginger, chopped

Directions:
Preheat the oven to 375 degrees Fahrenheit and prepare cookie sheets with parchment paper.

In a small bowl, mix the flour, wheat germ, baking soda, salt and ginger. Whisk well to combine.

In a large bowl, whisk the egg with the brown sugar, oil, chocolate, blueberries and crystallized ginger. Drop the cookie dough by using rounded tablespoons on 2 parchment covered cookie sheets spacing them 1/2 inch apart.

Bake the cookies for about 10 to 12 minutes or until they are puffed and golden brown. Cool for 2 minutes and lift onto a wire rack to cool completely.

CHERRY RICOTTA DESSERT

This recipe is almost like a pudding and is absolutely delicious. This recipe is so easy that you will find it hard to believe. The ricotta is packed with protein and the almonds and cherries give you extra energy. This recipe only makes one serving, so you better make enough for the whole family.

3/4 cup frozen, pitted cherries
2 tablespoons part-skim ricotta
1/4 teaspoon sweetener (stevia or other sweetener that can be heated)
1/4 teaspoon vanilla
1 tablespoon slivered, toasted almonds

Place the cherries in a microwave-safe bowl and cook on high until they are warm.

In a small bowl mix the ricotta with the sweetener and vanilla and drop it on top of the cherries. Sprinkle with the almonds and serve.

QUINOA APPLE CAKE

You know that old saying, "An apple a day keeps the doctor away"? Apples are a healthy fruit full of vitamins and fiber and they are considered an energy inducing food. Quinoa also pack energy as do some of the spices used in this recipe.

Ingredients:
1 cup quinoa

2 cups of water
1/2 cup wheat flour
1/2 cup all-purpose flour
1-1/2 teaspoon baking powder
2 apples, peeled and sliced
8 tablespoons salted butter, melted
3/4 cup brown sugar, packed
3/4 cup golden raisins
1 teaspoon ground cinnamon
1 teaspoon ground nutmeg
1 teaspoon ground ginger

Directions:
Preheat the oven to 305 degrees and spray a 9 by 5 inch loaf pan with non-stick spray.

In a small saucepan mix the quinoa with the water and bring it to a boil. Reduce the heat and simmer for 10 minutes or until the quinoa becomes tender and tails start to uncurl. Drain the quinoa and set it aside.

Dip a pastry brush in melted butter and grease the bottom and sides of the loaf pan.

Place the rest of the butter in a large bowl with the brown sugar, and raisins and mix to combine well. Add the apples and cooked and drained quinoa.

In a small bowl whisk both of the flours, baking powder and ground spices. Add to the wet ingredients and stir well. Place the batter into the loaf pan and bake 50 to 60 minutes or until toothpick inserted in center comes out clean and top is lightly browned. Cool 10 minutes and turn out to a cooling rack. Let the cake cool completely until cutting into slices.

QUICK SNACKS

The following snacks don't really need a recipe, but do have a procedure. All of them use energy foods to make something that will keep you awake and energized through the day in a healthy manner.

RICE CAKE SNACK
Spread 8 mini apple-cinnamon rice cakes with about 1 tablespoon peanut butter. Place one rice cake on a plate and top with a slice of banana. Top with another rice cake and another banana slice and then top with a rice cake. This makes 2 stacks.

YOGURT TREAT
Sprinkle some unsweetened dry cereal on a cup of yogurt and eat. The yogurt has protein that will get you through until the next meal and the cereal has carbs that satisfy and make it crunchy.

RED PEPPERS AND HUMMUS
Pick up some ready-made hummus and dip sliced red peppers in and eat. The hummus is filled with protein and the red peppers give you energy.

NUTS

All nuts have energy producing qualities and you can eat a handful of one type or a mixture of several to give you some good energy. Nuts also provide Omega 3's that give you energy. Do not eat too many because they do contain fat too.

COTTAGE CHEESE AND FRUIT
Place 1/2 cup cottage cheese in a bowl and top with 1/2 cup of fruit or apple sauce.

EDAMAME PODS
Edamame is filled with protein and offers a great deal of energy. One cup of edamame provides 17 grams of protein and that is a lot. Just stem fresh pods for about 6 minutes or microwave frozen for 2 minutes. Remove from pods before eating.

MASHED BLACK BEAN TACO
Put 1/2 cup black beans in a small microwave safe bowl with 1 tablespoon of salsa. Microwave about 1 minute until warm and mash with a fork. Place inside a 4 inch flour tortilla, fold over and eat or take several to work and eat cold for an energy pick up.

DELI ROLL
Layer some thin deli meat and cheese on a tortilla shell and sprinkle with some lettuce and top with a thin sliced tomato. Roll up and eat whole or cut into slices.

These recipes should provide you with many different satisfying, healthy and energy laden snacks that will give you something different for weeks.

Chapter 4 - Easy, Quick and Healthy Dinners

By the time dinner rolls around, you've already consumed some great energy laden meals and you should have enough pep left after work to do some cooking. Often times people skip either breakfast or lunch and by the time dinner time arrives, they have no energy left to cook dinner. So, where do they go for dinner? The fast food restaurant and the food there doesn't provide much energy. Dinner should be enough to satisfy hunger, but not so heavy as to keep you up late at night. Eat dinner no later than 4 hours before bedtime so the food has time to digest before lying down in bed. High energy dinners will not keep you up at night, but should supply enough to get you through six to eight hours of sleep without letting your blood sugar fall. The following recipes should do just that.

POULTRY RECIPES

COCONUT CHICKEN AND RICE
This chicken dish is a little sweet and very crispy. Even the kids will love it. It has whole wheat panko crumbs and some Basmati white rice, but you can always substitute brown rice. Brown rice just takes a little longer to cook. You do use all-purpose flour, but there isn't much added to the recipe. This recipe makes 4 to 6 servings

Ingredients:

Non-stick butter flavored cooking spray
1 pound chicken breast, boneless and skinless
½ cup whole wheat panko crumbs
½ cup coconut, sweetened and shredded
1/3 cup all-purpose flour
1 large egg
1 large egg white
Salt and black pepper to taste
6 cups of water
½ teaspoon salt
2 cups Basmati white rice
1-1/2 cups cream of coconut

Directions:
Preheat the oven to 400 degrees F and spray a baking pan or dish with the butter flavored non-stick spray.

Season the chicken with salt and pepper on both sides and set aside. In a small bowl, mix the panko crumbs and coconut. In another bowl, whisk the egg and egg white together until frothy. In a third bowl, place the flour.

Dip each chicken breast into the flour and shake to remove excess. Dunk it into the egg combination and then the coconut mixture. Place the breasts on the baking sheet or dish.

Bake for about 30 to 35 minutes, making sure to flip over halfway through. The chicken breasts should be a golden, crispy brown.

Meanwhile, cook the rice by bringing the water with the ½ teaspoon of salt to a boil in a saucepan. When it starts to bubble, reduce the heat to medium and add ½ cup of the cream of coconut. Stir, let it dissolve and add the rice. Cook the rice uncovered for 15 minutes at a rolling boil.

When rice is almost done, add the rest of the cream of coconut and stir well. Turn the heat to low and simmer for 5 minutes. Serve with the chicken,

HERB LEMON CHICKEN

This recipe makes 4 servings and you might want to make a little more for leftovers. The olive oil and citrus in this recipe make it very healthy and energy laden.

Ingredients:
4 tablespoons olive oil + 2 teaspoons more
4 large chicken breast halves
Juice and zest of 2 lemons
½ cup fresh parsley
½ cup fresh mint leaves
½ cup fresh basil leaves
Salt and pepper to taste
½ cup white wine

Directions:
Preheat the oven to 400 degrees F.

In an oven-proof skillet, heat up 3 tablespoons of the olive oil over high heat and sear the chicken on both sides for 2 minutes on each side. Place the skillet in the preheated oven and cook for about 8 minutes.

In a blender or food processor, process the rest of the oil, lemon juice, lemon zest and herbs by pulsing until well combined. Set aside.

Remove the skillet from the oven and place the chicken breasts on a serving plate. Season them with salt and pepper.

Pour the wine into the hot skillet and scrape up all the brown bits for the bottom. Add the herb mixture to the skillet and cook on medium heat for about 1 minute stirring constantly. Pour the sauce over the chicken and serve.

ORANGE-GINGER CHICKEN WITH VEGETABLES IN A BOWL

This dish serves 4 and is only a mere 289 calories per serving. It has energy inducing orange and red pepper along with some broccoli and is served with brown rice. It makes your mouth water while you cook it because it smells so good and it is served in a bowl for easy eating. The recipe calls for fresh squeezed juice, but you can substitute unsweetened orange juice in a bottle or can. Avoid sugary concentrated orange juice or you will defeat the energy purpose.

Ingredients:
2 cloves garlic, minced
3 tablespoons soy sauce, reduced-sodium
2 tablespoons fresh orange juice
1 tablespoon, fresh gingers, minced
1 pound chicken breasts, skinless, boneless and thinly sliced
½ teaspoon canola oil, divided
4 green onions, sliced thin
1 red bell pepper, sliced thin
1 cup fresh broccoli florets (use frozen ones thawed and drained if desired)
1 tablespoon of water
1 tablespoon sesame seed
2 cups brown rice, cooked

Directions:
In a large bowl, combine the garlic, soy sauce, orange juice and ginger. Whisk it together well and add the chicken pieces tossing them to coat. Put the bowl in the refrigerator, covered, for about 15 minutes or longer.

Heat up a wok or large skillet over medium heat. Pour the canola oil in a spray bottle and spritz the skillet two times. Cook the onions, peppers, and broccoli and then add the water. Stir fry for 4 to 5 minutes or until they are tender. Place in a bowl and set aside.

Spritz the skillet with 2 more spritzes of oil. Pick up the chicken from the marinade with a slotted spoon and put in the hot skillet. Cook for 4 minutes and stirring frequently. Add the vegetables, the marinade and sesame seeds and stir fry about 2 minutes.

Divide the hot cooked rice between 4 serving bowls. Large cereal bowls will do nicely. Divide the chicken and vegetable mixture between the bowls and serve steaming hot.

TURKEY CHILI WITH KALE

Kale is a dark green vegetable that infuses the body with energy. There are also black beans and fiber rich corn in the recipe to supply more energy. It may seem like there are too many ingredients to be simple, but it is really easy to make and tastes wonderful. This recipe makes 8 1-cup servings.

Ingredients:
1 tablespoon olive oil
1-1/2 pounds lean ground turkey (you can also use chicken)
1 teaspoon salt
1 teaspoon pepper
1 medium onion, diced
2 cloves garlic, minced
2 tablespoons tomato paste
1 tablespoon brown sugar
1 tablespoon chili powder
1 teaspoon cumin
1 teaspoon dried oregano
1 – 28 ounce can diced tomatoes

2 cups chicken broth
½ bunch (about 4 ounces) kale, stems removed and leaves chopped into ribbons
1 – 15 ounce can black beans, drained and rinsed
1 cup frozen corn kernels

Directions:

In a Dutch oven, add some of the olive oil and heat over medium heat. Add the turkey, salt and pepper and heat about 6 to 8 minutes. Break the turkey up with a wooden spoon so it crumbles. Place the meat in a holding bowl with a slotted spoon.

Drain all but 1 tablespoon of the fat in the pan (if there is no fat add 1 tablespoon olive oil.) Increase the heat to medium and cook the onions until softened, about 5 minutes. Add the garlic and heat about 30 seconds. Add tomato paste, sugar, chili powder, cumin, oregano and cook for 2 minutes stirring to combine the ingredients. Add the tomatoes, stir and heat.

Combine the ground turkey with the broth and increase heat to medium high. Bring to a simmer and cook 20 minutes.

Add the kale, beans and corn and cook until kale is soft and tender, but still looks green. This will take about 8 to 10 minutes. Add more salt or pepper if desired.

BEEF AND PORK

Contrary to popular belief, you can eat beef and pork in moderation, be healthy and have lots of energy. Beef and pork both contain protein and are good for you as long as you choose lean meat without too much fat.

UNSTUFFED PEPPERS

Green peppers are full of nutrients, but if use red peppers, you are giving your body an energy boost. This is a dish made entirely in a skillet. Use ground beef that is 90 to 95 percent lean to make 4 large servings.

Ingredients:
1 teaspoon olive oil
2 pounds ground beef
1 clove garlic, crushed
1 medium onion, chopped
1 red pepper, seeded and chopped
1 – 28 ounce can of crushed tomatoes
1/4 teaspoon salt
1/4 teaspoon pepper
1 teaspoon paprika
2 cups cooked brown rice

Directions:
Over medium heat, heat a skillet and add the olive oil. Immediately put the beef in the skillet and stir continuously to break it up and brown the meat.

Once the meat is browned, remove it from the skillet using a slotted spoon and set aside. Leave about 1 – 1/2 teaspoons of the fat in the skillet. If there is none, add another 1 – 1/2 teaspoons of olive oil.

Add the garlic, onion and red pepper. Cook and stir over medium heat until the vegetables become soft, about 5 to 8 minutes. Place the browned ground beef back in the skillet and add the crushed tomatoes, salt, pepper and paprika. Stir well.

Add the rice and when the mixture starts to boil, turn the heat to simmer for 10 minutes. Serve hot.

RAINBOW PEPPER STEAK

This recipe makes 4 servings of an Asian inspired dish and uses very little beef and a whole lot of vegetables. If you cannot get shiitake mushrooms, you can use baby portabellas. The star of this recipe is the pepper, which is a high energy food.

Ingredients:
1/2 pound lean flank steak
1-1/2 teaspoon cornstarch
1 tablespoon + 1 teaspoon dry sherry
1 teaspoon low sodium soy sauce
2 cloves garlic, minced
1/4 teaspoon sea salt
1/2 teaspoon ground pepper
1 teaspoon cold water
1 teaspoon sesame oil

2 tablespoons peanut oil
1 tablespoon fresh ginger, minced
1/2 teaspoon red pepper flakes
8 ounces shiitake mushrooms, stems removed and caps quartered
1 red bell pepper, seeded and chopped
1 green bell pepper, seeded and chopped
1 orange bell pepper, seeded and chopped
1 purple bell pepper, seeded and chopped
1 Anaheim pepper, seeded and chopped
2 tablespoons hoisin sauce

Directions:
Slice the flank steak into 2 inch wide strips with the grain. Cut the strips across the grain into slices that are 1/4 inch thick. In a bowl mix the cornstarch, 1 teaspoon of the sherry, soy sauce, one of the garlic cloves that has been minced, salt, pepper, cold water and sesame oil. Add the beef slices and coat well.

In a small bowl, mix the rest of sherry and hoisin sauce. Set aside for use later.

Heat the wok over high. Drop some water into the wok and when it evaporates within a few seconds, swirl in 1 tablespoon of the peanut oil and brown the beef making sure not to overlap it. Wait for about 1 minute before you begin to stir. Stir fry for 1 minute and remove the beef to a plate.

Swirl more of the peanut oil into the wok adding the rest of the garlic with the ginger, red pepper flakes and stir fry for 10 seconds. Add the mushrooms and peppers and stir fry for 2 minutes. Put the meat back in the wok with the hoisin sauce and fry stirring about 1 minute or until the strips are cooked through. Serve with brown rise or oriental noodles.

SAUSAGE, LENTIL AND KALE SKILLET DINNER

Using chicken sausage reduces the fat and the lentils and kale supply the body with energy. This recipe is super easy and makes 4 servings that taste spicy and delicious.

Ingredients:
3 teaspoons olive oil
1 -12 ounce package cooked chicken sausage
1 large onion, sliced thin
1 onion, peeled and sliced thin
1 pinch red pepper flakes
2-1/2 cups water
1-1/2 cups red wine
1 cup lentils
12 cups kale, stems removed and chopped
1 teaspoon fresh sage leaves chopped
1/4 teaspoon salt
1/4 teaspoon pepper

Directions:

Place 1 teaspoon of the olive oil in a skillet over medium heat. Add sausage and brown for 4 to 5 minutes and drain on paper towels.

Add the remaining olive oil in the skillet and brown the onion for 4 minutes. Stir in the garlic and red pepper flakes stirring for 30 seconds. Add the water and wine and bring the heat up to high. When it begins to boil, scrape up the brown bits on the bottom of the pan and add the lentils. Reduce to simmer, cover and cook 30 to 40 minutes.

Add the kale, sage, salt and pepper and cover to cook, stirring occasionally until the kale and lentils are tender, for about 10 more minutes.

Slice the cooked sausage into thin slices and add. Heat through for 2 minutes and serve.

FISH AND SEAFOOD DISHES

Fish and seafood is high in omega-3's, which is a fatty acid that body needs to function correctly. Omega-3 is not produced in the body, so the body has to get it from outside sources. Fish is the perfect food to provide this substance and salmon is very high in omega-3's.

LEMON SALMON

Citrus gives the body energy and so does salmon, so this is a win, win recipe. This recipe makes 4 servings and is put in the broiler to cook, so it is very quick to make.

Ingredients:
4 – 6 ounce salmon fillets
1/4 teaspoon sea salt
1/2 teaspoon fresh ground pepper
1-1/2 teaspoon grated lemon rind
3 tablespoons fresh squeezed lemon juice, divided
2 tablespoons olive oil, divided
1 teaspoon dried rosemary
Vegetable cooking spray
2 cups hot cooked brown rice
4 cups baby spinach

Directions:
Sprinkle the salmon with salt and pepper and put them in a closeable storage bag with the lemon rind, 1 tablespoon of the lemon juice and 1 tablespoon of the oil. Close and squish around. Refrigerate 30 minutes to overnight.

Line a pan with aluminum foil and spray it with the cooking spray. Remove the fillets and place them on the broiler skin side down. Discard the marinade. Broil the fish about 5-1/2 inches away from the flame. Cook 10 to 12 minutes or until the fish is flaky.

Arrange the rice and baby spinach on a serving platter. Top with the cooked fillets.

In a small bowl, whisk together the rest of the lemon juice and olive oil. Drizzle this over the fish and serve.

HERB ENCRUSTED SALMON AND VEGETABLE SALAD

The salmon is a healthy dish and pair it with a mixed green and vegetable salad and you have a great energy dinner. This recipe makes 4 servings.

Ingredients:
1/2 cup dried whole wheat bread crumbs
2 teaspoons fresh oregano, chopped
2 teaspoons fresh rosemary, chopped
2 teaspoons fresh parsley, chopped
1-1/2 teaspoons grated lemon rind
1/4 teaspoons ground pepper
2 garlic cloves, minced
4 – 6 ounce salmon fillets about 1 inch thick without skin
Sea salt
Butter flavored non-stick spray
1 tablespoon fresh squeezed lemon juice
1 tablespoon olive oil
1 teaspoon Dijon mustard
1/4 teaspoon sea salt
1/4 teaspoon pepper
4 cups mixed greens
1 cup cherry tomatoes, halved
1 zucchini, sliced and quartered
1 cucumber, sliced with skin on

Directions:
In a pie plate combine the crumbs, herbs, lemon rind, pepper and garlic. Spray both sides of the fillets with nonstick spray and dredge into the bread crumb combination.

Heat a skillet over medium heat. Turn off the heat and spray a thick layer of the butter flavored nonstick spray. Add the fillets, turn the burner to medium and cook for 3 minutes. Turn down to medium and carefully flip the fillets. Cook for 4 minutes or until the fish flakes easily.

In a small bowl combine the lemon juice, olive oil, mustard, salt and pepper. Whisk well. In a salad bowl combine the greens, tomatoes, zucchini and cucumber and pour the dressing in the bowl over top. Toss well and serve the salad alongside the salmon.

SCALLOPS WITH WHITE BEANS AND SPINACH

Talk about energy meals, this one has white beans for extra protein and spinach for iron. Not only does it pack an energy punch, but it is delicious too.

Ingredients:
2 strips turkey bacon, chopped in small pieces
1/2 red onion, minced
1 clove garlic, minced
1-1/2 (14 ounce) cans of white cannallini beans, rinsed and drained

4 cups baby spinach
1 pound large sea scallops
Salt and pepper to taste
1 tablespoon butter
Juice of 1 lemon

Directions:

Fry the bacon until crisp in a large skillet. Drain on paper towel on a plate. Add the onion and garlic to the skillet and sauté until the onion is tender, for 2 to 3 minutes. Add the beans and spinach and cook until beans are heated through and spinach is wilted. Keep this mixture warm.

Place another skillet on the burner, preferably a cast iron one, and heat it up. Blot the scallops off using a paper towel so they are dry and season with salt and pepper on both sides. In the skillet, melt the butter and add the scallops. Sear 2 to 3 minutes each side. They should look brown being caramelized.

Right before servings, squeeze the lemon juice to the bean mixture and stir in well. Season with salt and pepper. Divide the mixture between four bowls and place the scallops on top.

PASTA

Pasta contributes to the carbohydrate count of recipes, but if you use whole wheat or whole grain pasta, the carbs are drastically reduced and you are adding fiber to your diet. It is hard to avoid pasta dishes because the kids love them and they are really easy to make. Make your pasta a little more healthy and energy producing with the following recipes.

PESTO PASTA

In this recipe, you make your own pesto, but it isn't hard if you have a food processor or blender. Pine nuts are an ingredient, but sometimes they are hard to find and expensive. You can substitute almonds. You can use any type of wheat pasta from spaghetti to penne. This recipe makes 6 to 8 servings.

Ingredients:
1 pound whole wheat or whole grain pasta
2 cups fresh basil leaves, packed
1/3 cup pine nuts
2 garlic cloves, chopped
3/4 cup extra virgin olive oil
1/2 cup fresh grated Parmesan cheese
salt and pepper to taste

Directions:
Cook pasta in a large pot full of water until it is al dente.

Meanwhile, place the basil and nuts in a food processor or heavy duty blender and pulse 3 or 4 times. Add the garlic and pulse 3 or 4 more times.

Turn the processor on and slowly drizzle the oil in. Stop to scrape down the sides a few times so it all gets mixed in. Add the cheese, salt and pepper and pulse the mixture a few times for it to combine.

Drain the pasta and place it in a big pasta bowl. Pour the pesto over top and mix to combine. Sprinkle with a little more grated Parmesan.

SPAGHETTI AND TURKEY MEATBALLS
Everyone likes a good spaghetti and meatball dinner on occasion. This one is made with turkey and whole wheat pasta and should satisfy your craving for Italian food in a healthy way that gives you some great energy. Flaxseed is used in the recipe and it provides the body with a source of fiber and Omega 3's. This recipe makes 4 servings.

Ingredients:
8 ounces whole wheat spaghetti
1 pound ground turkey
2 tablespoons ground flaxseed
3 tablespoons grated Parmesan cheese
1 large egg, beaten
1 teaspoon salt
1/2 teaspoon ground pepper
2 tablespoons olive oil, divided
4 cloves garlic, peeled and minced
2 pounds ripe tomatoes, chopped or 2 – 28 ounce cans crushed tomatoes
1/4 to 1/2 teaspoon crushed red pepper flakes

1 teaspoon Italian seasonings
1 teaspoon sugar (optional)

Directions:

Cook the pasta as per the package directions to al dente. Save 3 tablespoons of the water and drain off the rest.

While the pasta is cooking, in a large bowl, mix the turkey, flaxseed, Parmesan, egg, 1/2 teaspoon of the salt and all the pepper. Combine well using your hands and form into meatballs.

Heat a skillet to medium high and add in 1 tablespoon of the oil. Drop the meatballs in the skillet and roll them around to brown on all sides. Work in small batches and place browned meatballs on a plate or in a dish. You do not have to cook them all the way through. Browning should only take about 10 minutes.

In the same skillet, add the rest of the olive oil and pour in the onions. Sauté until they are softened and slightly browned. Sauté the garlic for about 10 seconds. Add the tomatoes, pepper flakes, Italian seasoning and the sugar, if desired. Bring the mixture to a boil and add the meatballs and the other 1/2 teaspoon salt. Bring heat to a simmer, cover and let cook 10 minutes stirring occasionally.

Place the drained pasta in a bowl along with the 3 tablespoons reserved liquid. Pour the sauce over top and toss. Sprinkle it with more Parmesan cheese and serve.

BONUS MEALS

POWER HOUSE HAWAIIAN PIZZA

Hawaiian pizza traditionally has a red sauce, cheese, ham and pineapple chunks. The pineapple gives it some extra zip and supplies vitamins. You can get a whole wheat pizza shell to make this recipe or you can make your own whole wheat pizza since the shells are sometimes hard to find. Use the dough and make other types of pizza besides a Hawaiian variety as per the tips below the recipe. This recipe makes a 12 ounce pizza which is commonly cut in 8 pieces.

DOUGH

Ingredients:
3/4 cup whole wheat flour
3/4 cup all-purpose flour
1 package or 2-1/4 teaspoon quick rising yeast
1/2 teaspoon salt
1/4 teaspoon sugar
1/2 to 2/3 cup hot water
2 teaspoons olive oil

Directions:

In a food processor, combine both of the flours, yeast, salt and sugar. Pulse to combine.

Place 1/2 cup of the hot water in a 4 cup measuring cup and add the olive oil. While the processor is running, slowly pour the water oil mixture in. It should form into a sticky, soft ball. If the ball is dry, add the rest of the water to make a total of 2/3 cup. If it gets too sticky, add 1 to 2 tablespoons more of flour. Once the ball forms, process for 1 minute to knead.

Sprinkle a clean cutting board with flour and spread it out. Place the dough on the board and cover it with plastic wrap sprayed with nonstick spray, sprayed side down. Leave the dough rise for 20 minutes. Roll the dough in a circle or rectangle and finish making the pizza as desired.

SAUCE:

Ingredients:
4 Roma tomatoes, peeled and seeded
1/2 teaspoon Italian seasonings
1/2 teaspoon basil
1/2 teaspoon fennel seed
1/4 teaspoon salt
1/2 teaspoon red pepper flakes
1/2 teaspoon olive oil
1/2 teaspoon garlic, minced
1/2 teaspoon brown sugar

Directions:
Pulse the tomatoes in a food processor or blender with the rest of the ingredients. Processes the mixture until it becomes smooth and pour it into a saucepan. Bring the sauce to a boil and immediately turn it down to a simmer for 20 minutes or until the sauce reduces by half.

TOPPINGS:
4 slices deli ham, cut in strips or 4 slices bacon
3/4 cup mozzarella cheese
1/4 cup red onion, diced
1 cup pineapple tidbits drained

CONSTRUCTION:
Place the rolled dough on a baking sheet covered with foil and sprayed with non-stick spray. Spread the sauce on the dough.

In a skillet, brown the ham strips or cook the bacon until cooked and still pliable. Tear the meat into pieces.

Sprinkle the cheese over the sauce on the pizza and then scatter the meat, red onion and pineapple on top. Put in a preheated 450 degree oven for about 14 minutes or until the crust is just browned.

OTHER POWERHOUSE PIZZAS

PESTO PIZZA

Make the whole wheat pizza crust and drizzle and spread with just enough olive oil to make the surface wet. Spread on a healthy dollop of pesto and top with sliced onion, thinly sliced tomato and Parmesan cheese.

MARGHERITA PIZZA

Spread a little olive oil on the pizza crust and put down a layer of diced onion, another layer of grated Parmesan cheese mixed with a little dried oregano, and another layer of thinly sliced tomatoes. Either sprinkle a little shredded mozzarella cheese on top or slice it thin and place it on top. Sprinkle on some fresh basil leaves and bake.

VEGGIE PIZZA

Spread the above sauce on the pizza crust and top. Steam some broccoli, cauliflower and carrot slices for about 5 minutes to soften them. Place them on the pizza along with some thinly sliced onion. Sprinkle either mozzarella or shredded cheddar on top and bake.

SWEET POTATO BURRITO

Sweet potatoes are an energy food and these burritos are unexpected and very good. You will get fiber and many different vitamins and minerals with this dish. The avocado is also a great source of energy and many vitamins. This recipe makes about 4 to 8 burritos depending on the size of the tortillas.

Ingredients:
1 tablespoon olive oil
1 large onion, chopped
1 clove garlic, minced
1 teaspoon curry powder
2 teaspoons cumin
1 large sweet potato, grated
1 teaspoon chili powder
1 to 2 teaspoons water
salt and pepper to taste
2 cups black beans, rinsed and drained
1-1/2 cup of shredded Cheddar cheese
Salsa
1 avocado, sliced
Tortillas (whole wheat or flour)

Directions:
Turn the burner to medium high and heat a large skillet. Add the olive oil and cook the onions until they become translucent, about 2 or 3 minutes. Add the garlic, curry and cumin and sauté for a few seconds. Add the sweet potato and chili powder and mix together. Sauté for about 2 minutes stirring continuously.

Add water and salt and pepper to taste. Reduce the heat to low and simmer with a lid on the pot for 5 minutes or until the sweet potatoes are tender.

In another bowl, heat the beans in the microwave for 1 or 2 minutes. Also slice the avocado. Warm the tortillas in a 400 degree F oven for about 5 minutes.

Place individual tortillas on a flat surface and spread with the beans and the potato mixture. Sprinkle with cheese, a teaspoon of salsa and some avocado and roll. Serve warm.

For some vegetarian dinners that pack energy in every bite, see the video, 3 Dinner recipes for maximum weight loss & energy! from Freelee the Banana Girl.

Dinners that provide the body with energy actually help you sleep. Your sugar does not plummet and cause restlessness during the night. You wake up fresh and ready for the next day.

Conclusion

I hope this book was able to provide you with healthy and energy filled meals that you and your loved ones can enjoy for snacks, breakfast, lunch and dinner!

The next step is to try each recipe to see what you and your family enjoys. You can also keep a food journal to keep track of your energy levels and overall mood throughout the day, so that you can determine which recipes are ideal for your individual health. Feel free to experiment with the recipes and make them your own and remember that the foods that include fruits, vegetables, protein filled meats, beans, nuts, dairy products and fish are all great for your overall health. Keep a balanced diet by eating healthy and providing your body all the vitamins and minerals it needs to stay healthy and strong.

Finally, if you discovered at least one thing that has helped you or that you think would be beneficial to someone else, be sure to take a few seconds to easily post a quick positive review. As an author, your positive feedback is desperately needed. Your highly valuable five star reviews are like a river of golden joy flowing through a sunny forest of mighty trees and beautiful flowers! *To do your good deed in making the world a better place by helping others with your valuable insight, just leave a nice review.*

My Other Books and Audio Books
www.AcesEbooks.com

Health Books

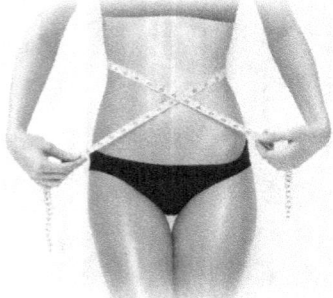

Peak Performance Books

Be sure to check out my audio books as well!

 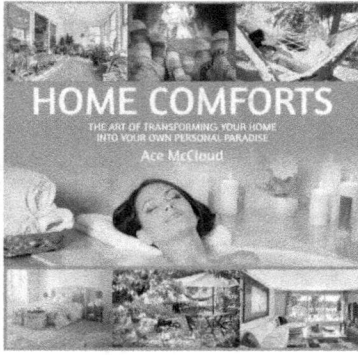 

Check out my website at: www.AcesEbooks.com for a complete list of all of my books and high quality audio books. I enjoy bringing you the best knowledge in the world and wish you the best in using this information to make your journey through life better and more enjoyable! **Best of luck to you!**

www.ingramcontent.com/pod-product-compliance
Lightning Source LLC
Chambersburg PA
CBHW051422070526
44584CB00023B/3539